At the Shops

Paul Humphrey

Photography by Chris Fairclough

W
FRANKLIN WATTS
LONDON • SYDNEY

First published in 2005 by
Franklin Watts
96 Leonard Street
London EC2A 4XD

Franklin Watts Australia
Level 17/207 Kent Street
Sydney NSW 2000

ISBN 0 7496 6178 X (hbk)
ISBN 0 7496 6190 9 (pbk)

Dewey classification number: 381'.1

A CIP catalogue record for this book is available
from the British Library.

Planning and production by Discovery Books Limited
Editor: Rachel Tisdale
Designer: Ian Winton
Photography: Chris Fairclough
Series advisors: Diana Bentley MA and Dee Reid MA
Fellows of Oxford Brookes University

The author, packager and publisher would like to thank the following
people for their participation in this book: Samiya and Lucsir Latif
and family; Focus Do-It-All and ASDA, Nottingham.

Printed in China

Contents

Dad and Samiya went shopping.

Shopping

Cheese
Milk
Eggs
Bread
Oranges
carrots
Sugar

4

On the way
to the shops,
they saw
Uncle Latif.

Please can you buy
me some nails?

6

First, they went to the supermarket.

Dad checked the shopping list.

They went to the bread counter.

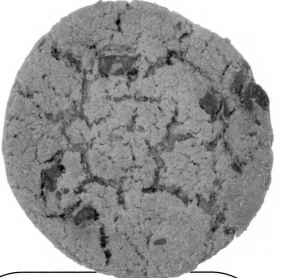

Can I have a cookie, please?

15

They finished the shopping and went to pay at the checkout.

ASDA Price

Always **LOW PRICES**

ASDA STORES LTD.
WWW.ASDA.COM

HYSON GREEN, 17 IR. 06628
ST. 4938 OP. 00000943 TE £0.99D
000002719378 £0.84D
2222 023211000034 £0.98D
COOKIES 5PK 000002743001 £0.54D
ORANGES 1KG 000002300350 £0.42D
CARROTS. 000002117238 £0.44D
WHT BAGUETTE 000002041536 £0.44D
BREAD 000002041536 £0.15V
BREAD 000008419655 £1.70D
CHUPA MAX 026058600170 £1.16D
S/P CHEDDAR 000002040846 £0.62D
S/PRICE EGGS 023003000062 £1.03D
WHOLEMEAL TN 000002033216 £1.78V
ASDA MILK 500015930825 £0.68D
MALTESERS 501006730150
SILVER SPOO

TOTAL £11.77
CASH £20.00
CHANGE DUE £8.23

17

Dad took the bags out of the trolley. He loaded them into the car.

Next, they went to the hardware shop.

21

Samiya gave Uncle Latif his hammer ...

... and enjoyed
her cookie!

23

Word bank

Look back for these words and pictures.

Checkout

Cookie

Eggs

Hammer

Hardware shop

Nails

Shopping list

Supermarket

Trolley